Charles Wentworth Dilke

The Fall of Prince Florestan of Monaco

Charles Wentworth Dilke

The Fall of Prince Florestan of Monaco

ISBN/EAN: 9783337105563

Printed in Europe, USA, Canada, Australia, Japan

Cover: Foto ©ninafisch / pixelio.de

More available books at **www.hansebooks.com**

OF

PRINCE FLORESTAN OF MONACO.

BY HIMSELF.

London:

MACMILLAN AND CO.

1874.

THE FALL

OF

PRINCE FLORESTAN OF MONACO.

I AM Prince Florestan of Wurtemberg, born in 1850, and consequently now of the mature age of twenty-four. I might call myself "FLORESTAN II." but I think it better taste for a dethroned prince, especially when he happens to be a republican, to resume the name that is in reality his own.

Although the events which I am about to relate occurred this winter, so little is known in England of the affairs of the Ex-principality of

B

Monaco, now forming the French commune of that name, that I feel that the details of my story; indeed all but the bare facts on which it is grounded, will be news to English readers. The English Post Office believes that Monaco forms part of Italy, and the general election extinguished the telegrams that arrived from France in February last.

All who follow continental politics are aware that the Prince Charles Honoré, known as Charles III. of Monaco, and also called on account of his infirmity "the blind prince," was the ruling potentate of Monaco during the last gambling season; that there lived with him his mother, the dowager princess; that he was a widower with one son, Prince Albert, Duc de Valentinois, heir apparent to the throne; that the latter had by his marriage with the Princess Marie of Hamilton, sister to the Duke of Hamilton, one son who in 1873 was six years old; that all the family lived on M. Blanc the lessee of the gambling tables. But Monaco is shut off from the rest of the world except in the winter months, and few have heard of the calamities which since the end of January have rained upon the ruling family. My cousin, Prince Albert, the "Sailor Prince," a good fellow of my own age, with no fault but his rash love of uselessly braving the perils of the ocean, had often been warned of the fate that would one day befall him. Once when a boy he had put to sea in his boat when a fearful storm was raging, had been upset just off the point at Monaco, and had been saved only by the gallantry of a sailor of the port who had risked his own life in keeping his sovereign's son afloat. In October 1873 my unfortunate cousin bought at Plymouth an English sailing yacht of 450 tons. He had a sailor's contempt for steam, which he told me was only fit for lubbers, when he came up and stayed with me at Cambridge in November to see the "fours." He explained to me then that he had got a bargain, that he had bought his yacht for one-third her value, and that he was picking up a capital crew of thirty men. He had no need to buy yachts for a third their value, for he was rich enough and to spare, having enjoyed the large fortune of his mother from the time he came of age. She was a Mérode, and vast forests in Belgium—part of Soignies for instance—belonged to him. His wife had her own fortune of four and a half million francs, bringing her in about seven thousand pounds a year, so he was able to spend all his money on himself. He did not spend it on his dress, for when he came to Cambridge and was introduced to Dr. Thompson, he neither had a dress suit to dine in at the lodge, nor a black morning coat to put on for hall, where his rough pea-jacket scandalised the "scouts." He sailed from Plymouth in November, and reached Monaco at the end of that month. In December he made several excursions, in none of which did his father go to sea with him, but on the 26th of January, as ill luck would have it, he tempted my poor uncle to go with him for a three days, cruise. It came on to blow hard that night, and nothing was ever heard of them again. Great was the excitement at Monaco on the 27th and 28th, but on the 29th the worst was known, as a telegram from Genoa informed the unfortunate old princess—who has all her faculties at the age of eighty-six—that her son and grandson were both numbered with the dead, for one of the boats of the rotten yacht had been fallen in with by a fishing vessel floating empty in mid sea.

The Conseil d'Etat was at once called together by the Governor General, and the little boy of the Princess Marie proclaimed by their order at the market-place. A proclamation was posted in the town the moment the sitting ended, declaring the joint regency of the dowager princess and of Baron Imberty. A telegram was sent to Princess Marie, who was staying with her child at Nice, informing her of her husband's death and of the accession of her son, and begging that she would the next day confide the little Duc de Valentinois to the deputation of the councillors of state and of the officers of guards, who would reach Nice by train at noon. She was in the same despatch assured that on the death of the old dowager princess she should succeed her in the regency, but for family reasons on which I need not enlarge, she was requested not on this occasion to accompany her son.

All this I learnt by a telegram from the baron; I, as the son of the sister of the late prince, having now become most unexpectedly next heir to the throne of Monaco. I had no idea of the possibility of my ever being called upon to succeed a healthy boy of six, and gave the matter no thought but one of regret at the death of my gallant cousin Albert, who in the Prussian war had proved his courage in the French navy, while I, had I been older, should have had to have fought upon the other side, my father having been a prince of Wurtemberg.

I was thoroughly English in my ways. My father, a man of wide and liberal views, disliking "professors" as much as Mr. Disraeli does, and especially distrusting Prussian peda-

gogues, had sent me to Eton and to Trinity.
At Eton I had lived rather with the King's
scholars than with my more natural allies, and
had imbibed some views at which my poor
father would have groaned. When I went up
to Cambridge my friendships were in King's
rather than in Third Trinity, and my opinions
were those now popular among spectacled under-
graduates, namely, universal negation. I even
joined First Trinity Boat Club, instead of Third,
because the gentlemen of the latter were too
exclusive for my princely tastes.

During my four years at Cambridge I had
rowed in First Trinity Second. I had heard at
the Union Mr. Seeley defend the Commune, and
oppose a motion declaring it innocent because
it did not go on to express the "love and
affection" with which that body was regarded
by the University. I had supported a young

fellow of Trinity when he showed that the surplus funds of the Union Society should be
applied to the erection of statues of Mazzini
in all the small villages of the West of England
—a motion which I believe was carried, but
neutralized by the fact that the Union Society
possessed no surplus funds. I had also had the
inestimable advantage of attending the lectures
of Professor Fawcett on the English poor laws.
I had, by the way, almost forgotten the most
amusing of all the Union episodes of my time,
which was the rising of Mr. Dilke of Trinity
Hall, Sir Charles Dilke's brother—but a man
of more real talent than his brother, although,
if possible, a still more lugubrious speaker—to
move that his brother's portrait, together with
that of Lord Edmond Fitzmaurice, the com-
munist brother of a Marquis and a congenial
spirit, should be suspended in the committee

room to watch over the deliberations of that
body, because, forsooth, they had happened to
be president and vice-president of the Society
at a moment when the new buildings were begun
out of the subscriptions of such very different
politicians as the Prince of Wales, the Duke of
Devonshire, and Lord Powis. Mr. Dilke and
his radicals were sometimes in a majority and
sometimes in a minority at the Union, and the
portraits of the republican lord and baronet went
up on the wall or down under the table accord-
ingly, Mr. Willimott, the valued custodian of
the rooms, carrying out the orders of both sides
with absolute impartiality.

Fired with the enthusiasm of my party and
of my age, I had subscribed to the Woman's
Suffrage Association, to Mr. Bradlaugh's election
expenses, to the Anti-Game-Law Association, and
to the Education League. My reading was less

one-sided than my politics, and my republicanism was tempered by an unwavering worship of "Lothair." Mr. Disraeli was my admiration as a public man—a Bismarck without his physique and his opportunities—but then in politics one always personally prefers one's opponents to one's friends. As a republican, I had a cordial aversion for Sir Charles Dilke, a clever writer, but an awfully dull speaker, who imagines that his forte is public speaking, and who, having been brought up in a set of strong prejudices, positively makes a merit to himself of never having got over them. This he calls "never changing his opinions." For Mr. Gladstone I had the ordinary undergraduate detestation. There are no liberals at Cambridge. We were all rank republicans or champions of right divine.

The 31st of January was a strange day in my history. On entering my rooms in my flannels, hot from the boats, and hurrying for hall, I saw a telegram upon the table. I tore it open.

> " *The Governor-General, Monaco ;*
>
> *to*
>
> *His Serene Highness Prince Florestan,*
>
> *Trinity College,*
>
> *Cambridge.*"

"His Serene Highness!" Surely a mistake I read on.

"This morning at noon his Serene Highness the reigning prince was committed by the princess his mother to the care of M. Henri de Payan, at Nice. The princess being nervous about rail-way accidents, the departure for Monaco took place by road. The carriage conveying his Serene Highness and M. de Payan was drawn by four horses. Turbie was reached without mishap, but

half-way between Turbie and Roquebrune, at a
sharp turn in the road, the horses took fright,
and the coachman, in avoiding the precipice,
threw the carriage upon the rocks on the moun-
tain side of the road. His Serene Highness was
thrown on his head and killed on the spot.
Your Serene Highness is now reigning prince of
Monaco, and will be proclaimed to-night after
the meeting of the Council of State by the style
of Florestan II. Lieutenant Gasignol, of the
guard, will proceed at once to England and meet
your Serene Highness at any spot which your
Highness may please to indicate. M. de Payan
escaped without a scratch."

Prince of Monaco! Prince of Monaco. And
I had seen Lafont in *Rabagas!* I was not a
"milk-and-water Rabagas," as Mr. Cole called Mr.
Lowe, when all the papers reported him to have
said "milk-and-water Rabelais," and the *Spectator*

mildly wondered at the strangeness of the com-
parison. No, but I was somewhat of a milk-
and-water Prince of Monaco after Lafont. What
distinction! What carriage! If the princes of
the earth were only like the princes of the stage,
there would be no republicans. But then, fortunately, they are not. " Fortunately! " and I
one of them. What am I saying?

Poor little fellow! How sad for his young
mother too. A reigning prince for nineteen hours,
and that outside of his own dominions and at
the age of six. A strange world! and a strange
world, for me too. A half-Protestant, half-free-
thinking, republican, German, Cambridge undergraduate, suddenly called to rule despotically
over a Catholic and Italian people. My succession, at least, would be undisputed. No one had
ever vowed that I " should never ascend the
throne—without a protest." One of the Gri-

maldis had a claim which was no doubt a just
one, my respected great uncle having been pro-
bably a usurper'; but Marshal MacMahon and
the Duc de Broglie would, I well knew, support
me, preferring even a German prince at Monaco
to an Italian. My succession, I repeat, was undisputed; but if anybody had taken the trouble
to dispute it, I can answer for it that they
would have been cheated out of their amuse-
ment, for I should willingly have resigned to
their charge so burdensome a toy. I was that
which the republican mayor of Birmingham, Mr.
Joseph Chamberlain, in his jocular speech pro-
posing the Prince of Wales' health at the mayor's
banquet, said that one of his friends had been
trying by argument to make the Prince—with,
"as yet," only "partial success"—a republican
King. I would have gone only to Monaco to
proclaim the republic had I not known that

the strange despotism—presided over not as a despotism should be by one clever despot, but by two stupid despots, the Dukes of Magenta and Broglie—which is called the French republic, would not permit the creation of a small model for herself in the middle of her commune of Roquebrune.

I was not sorry to leave Cambridge. My rooms in the new court overlooked Caius, where they had typhoid fever ; and between the fear of infection and the noise of the freshmen's wines in Trinity Hall, I was beginning to have enough of Cambridge. My bedmaker and tutor were the only people to whom I bid goodbye. The men were all in hall and out at wines, and I left notes for my friends instead of looking them up in their rooms. I caught my tutor as he was going into hall. I told him of the news, and I could see the idea of an invitation for next winter to the castle at Monaco pass through his mind as he assured me that my rule would be a blessing to my country, and that nothing could better fit me for a sceptre than the training of an English gentleman. He added, with a return of the grim humour of a don, that he supposed that as a sovereign prince I need scarcely "take an *exeat*." My poor old bedmaker, who had read the telegram in my absence from my room, called me "your imperial majesty" three times while she packed my shirts, but in half-an-hour I was off to London; and on the evening of the 3rd of February I met M. de Payan and Lieutenant Gasignol by appointment at the Grand Hotel at Paris.

From M. de Payan I obtained my first accurate ideas as to the State of Monaco. I found that I was not more independent under the supremacy of France than is the Emperor William

c

independent under the domination of Prince von Bismarck. I had not only the Code Napoléon, and a Council of State dressed in exact copies of their Versailles namesakes, but French custom-house officers levying French custom-house duties in my dominions. At the beginning of our conversation I had said to M. de Payan, "Between ourselves, and fearing though I do that like Charles I. of England I may be committing high treason against myself, I feel bound to tell you that my only ideas of my principality are derived from M. Sardou's *Rabagas*."

Why is it that inhabitants of small and isolated communities never can see a joke? M. de Payan, slightly drawing himself up and speaking with as much stiffness as he could assume towards his prince, gravely answered me, "Your Serene Highness is not aware, I presume, that *Rabagas* was a satire directed against France in her decline, and not against your Highness's principality."

M. Sardou wasting his hours on satirising Monaco. I will never joke again, I said to myself, unless I should suffer the modern fate of kings and be 'deposed.

"M. de Payan," I replied, "I am aware of what you say, and I was joking."

"We have no Gambettas at Monaco, your Highness; that is all I meant."

"Perhaps, Sir, the country would be happier if you had. Rabagas was not Gambetta, but Emile Olivier—not the man who never despaired of France, but the man who sacrificed his opinions to his advancement. I admire M. Gambetta, who is at this moment the first man in France, in my estimation, and the second political man in Europe. His figure will stand out in history, daubed as even it is with the mud that

French politicians are ceaselessly flinging at each other."

"M. Gambetta is, as your Serene Highness says, a man of extraordinary powers; but his father was a tradesman at Cahors, and is retired and lives at Nice, near your Serene Highness's dominions."

What more could I say? There was nothing to be made of M. de Payan.

On the 5th of February I reached Nice by the express, and after reading the telegram which announced the return of Mr. Gladstone by a discerning people as junior colleague to a gin distiller, was presented with an address by the Gambettist mayor at the desire of the legitimist préfêt. The mayor, being a red-hot republican in politics but a carriage-builder by trade, lectured me on the drawbacks of despotism in his address, but informed me in conversation afterwards that he had had the honour of building a Victoria for Prince Charles Honoré—which was next door to giving me his business card. The address, however, also assumed that the Princes of Monaco were suffered only by Providence to exist in order that the trade of Nice, the nearest large French town, might thrive.

In the evening at four we reached the station at Monaco, which was decked with the white flags of my ancestors. What a pity, was my thought, that M. de Chambord should not be aware that if he would come to stay with me at the castle he would live under the white flag to which he is so much attached all the days of his life. My reception was enthusiastic. The guards, in blue uniforms not unlike the Bavarian, but with tall shakoes instead of helmets, and similar to that which during the stoppage of the train at Nice I had rapidly put on, were

drawn up in line to the number of thirty-nine
—one being in hospital with a wart on his
thumb, as M. de Payan told me. What an
admirable centralisation that such a detail should
be known to every member of the administration!
Two drummers rolled their drums French fashion.
In front of the line were four officers, of whom—
one fat; Baron Imberty; the Vicar General; and
Père Pellico of the Jesuits of the Visitation,
brother as I already knew to the celebrated
Italian patriot, Silvio Pellico, of dungeon and
spider fame.

"Where is M. Blanc?" I cried to M. de Payan,
as we stopped, seeing no one not in uniform or
robes.

"M. Blanc," said M. de Payan, severely,
"though a useful subject of your Highness is
neither a member of the household of your
Highness, a soldier of His army, nor a function-

ary of His government. M. Blanc is in the crowd outside."

Had I ventured to talk slang to M. de Payan, of whom I already stood in awe, I should have replied, "Elle est *salée*, celle là ; puisque sans M. Blanc mon pays ne marcherait pas." But I held my tongue.

I have seen many amusing sights in the course of my short life. I have seen an Anglican clergyman dance the cancan—I have seen Lord Claud Hamilton, the elder, address the English House of Commons—I have watched with breathless interest the gesticulations of French orators in the tribune of the Assembly, when not a word could reach my ears through the din of Babel that their colleagues made. But the oddest sight I ever saw was the bow with which Colonel Jacquemet, conscious ever. at the glorious moment that history would not forget his name, assured me that "the devoted army of a Gallant and a Glorious Prince would follow him to the death, when Honour led and Duty called."

At this moment Père Pellico slipped round to my side and said, "A word with your Highness. A most unfortunate report has got abroad that your Highness is a heretic. What is to be done ?"

"I very much fear I am," I replied.

"But surely your Highness has never formally joined a Protestant body ?"

"Protestant ? Oh, no. I am a freethinker ; a follower of Strauss rather than of Dr. Cumming."

"How your Highness has relieved my mind ! Only a freethinker—but that is nothing. I feared that possibly your Highness might have suffered a perversion to some of the many schisms." He bowed and hurried off into the town, while

taking the arm of Baron Imberty I said, " Intro-
duce me to M. Blanc."

" Your Highness wishes that M. Blanc should
be presented to your Highness, but there are
three hundred and ten or three hundred and
twenty gentlemen who take precedence of M.
Blanc. Nevertheless, your Highness has only to
command."

" Well, then, touch my arm as we pass him in
the crowd, and I will speak to him informally."

My ideas of etiquette would have horrified
Madame von Biegeleben, the lady-in-waiting to
my poor mother; still, I was improving already,
as may be seen.

As we left the station building a little man
in black, who when he is twenty years older will
be as like M. Thiers in person as he already is
in tact, in power of talk, and in the combination
of a total absence of fixed opinions with a de-

cided manner, made a low bow, accompanied with the shrewdest smile .that I had seen.

"That," I. said, halting before him, "is M. Blanc. I am glad to have so early an opportunity of commencing an acquaintance, which I hope to improve."

"Your Serene Highness does me too much honour."

Thus I passed the man who played Haussmann to my Emperor, but who had the additional advantage which the costly baron of demolishing memory certainly did not possess, of being a magnificent source of revenue to my state.

Mounting the really fine horse that they had sent me down, and escorted by the sixteen mounted carbineers (who do police duty on foot in ordinary times at Monte Carlo and in the town), I rode off at a sharp trot by the winding road.

"Will your Serene Highness graciously please to go at a walk, for otherwise the guards will not have time to get up by the military road and to form again to receive your Highness at the *Place.*"

I did as I was bid, of course. Bouquets of violets were showered on me as we passed through the narrow street, and the scene on the public square in front of the castle was really fine. The sun was setting in glory over the Mediterranean in the west; on the north the Alpes Monégasques were beginning to take the deep red glow which nightly in that glorious climate they assume. On the east the palms at Monte Carlo stood out sharply against the deep still blue sky, and in the far distance the great waves of the ground swell were rolling in upon the coast towards Mentone and the Italian frontier, with thousands of bright white sea-gulls speckling the watery hills with dots of light. At the palace gate I was received by the old dowager princess. She bent and kissed my hand. I threw my arms round her neck and kissed her on both cheeks.

"That was kindly meant, Highness," she said, "but your Serene Highness is now the reigning prince, and in the presence of the mob your dignity must be kept up."

Passing the two great Suisses who, arrayed in gala costume, stood magnificently at the gate—but whose wages I afterwards discovered were supplemented by showing my bedroom when I was out to English tourists at a franc a head—we entered the grand courtyard, ascended the great stairs, and passed straight into the reception hall known as the Salle Grimaldi. There, standing on a dais, opposite to the magnificent fireplace and chimney-piece, with the baron at my side, I held a levee, and received the vicar-general, père de Don ; the

curé of the cathedral, l' abbé Ramin ; the chevalier
de Castellat, vice-president of the council of state ;
the chevalier Voliver, member of council of state,
and president of the council of public education ;
the Marquis de Bausset-Roquefort, president of
the high court of justice and member of the
council of state ; the treasurer-general, M. Lom-
bard; Monsignore Theuret, the first almoner of the
household ; Monsignore Ciccodicola, the honorary
almoner ; Colonel the Vicomte de Grandsaigne, my
first aide-de-camp; Major Pouget d'Aigrevaux, com-
mandant of the palace ; the two attachés of M.
de Payan in his office of secretary-general, MM.
Stephen Gastaldi and John Blanchi; my doctor,
M. Coulon, a leading member of the council of
education, and evidently a most intelligent man :
the curés of the six smaller churches ; the five
professors of the Jesuit college of La Visitation ;
three aides-de-camp ; the chef du cabinet ; the

chamberlain himself, who had introduced the others; and four officers of guards and one of carbineers, in addition to Colonel Jacquemet, whom I have already named. No conversation took place, and the presentations being over in five minutes, I got out in the garden before dark for a quiet stroll by myself before dinner.

I was struck by the scene. The tall palms, the giant tree geraniums blooming in masses down the great cliffs to the very edge of the dark blue sea, the feathery mimosas, the graceful pepper trees laden with crimson berries, the orange grove, the bananas fruiting and flowering at the same time, the passion flowers climbing against the rugged old castle walls, all were new to me— unused to the south, and brought up in Buckinghamshire, in Cambridgeshire, and in central Germany. The scene saddened me, I know not why, and I asked myself whether, with the odd combination of my opinions and my position, I could be of any use in the world except to bring monarchy into contempt. Here was I, a free-thinker, called upon to rule a people of bigoted Catholics through a Jesuit father — for I had already seen that Père Pellico was the real vice-king. Here was I, an ardent partisan of the doctrine of individuality, placed suddenly at the head of the most centralized administration in the world. What was to be done? Reform it? Yes, but no reformer has so ill a time of it as a reforming prince. Sadly I went in to a sad dinner *tête-à-tête* with my crape-covered great aunt in a gloomy room, and so to bed, convinced that unhappiness may co-exist with the possession of a hall porter as big as Mrs. Bischoffsheim's.

The next morning when I dreamily called for my coffee there was brought to me along with it a gigantic envelope sealed with soft wax stamped with my arms, and containing a terrific despatch of twenty-three pages. "Rapport Hebdomadaire." "Weekly report" of what, I asked myself. Why, I have but five thousand subjects —the same number that Octavia Hill rules in Marylebone with such success. I began to read.

"On Monday night a man named Marsan called the carbineer Fissori a fool. He was not arrested (see Order No. 1142 and correspondence 70, 10, 102), but a private report was addressed to the Council of State, on which the Secretary General decided to recommend that Marsan should be watched for a week; referred to the Sub-Committee on Public Order."

"M. Blanc on Tuesday visited the tunnel in the commune of Turbie (France) by which he hopes to obtain an additional water supply for the Casino. As M. Blanc had not had the courtesy to inform the secretarial office of his excursion it was impossible to send an agent to obtain details of what took place."

So on for twenty and more pages, the last informing me of the names of the fishing boats that had come in and gone out, of the time of sunrise, and of the fact that a private in my guards had caught a cold in his head.

It was unbearable. These formalities should be suppressed at once. The administration should be decentralised. I rang and sent to the secretarial office for M. de Payan. I addressed him thus :—

"I gather from this tedious document that my principality of five thousand persons possesses every appliance and every excrescence of civilized government except a parliament. The perfection of bureaucracy and of red tape has been reached in a territory one mile broad and five miles long. No doubt centralisation is less hurtful than it is elsewhere in a country so small that it is virtually all centre, but I intend that this state of things (for which you are in no way responsible) shall cease. In the first place kindly inform me of the facts. What are the expenses and what are the revenues of the state, and what is the number of its officials ?"

" There are, Sir," he answered, " including your household and the officers of your guards, one hundred and twenty-six functionaries in Monaco. There are sixty soldiers and carbineers, and there are one hundred and fifty unpaid consular and diplomatic representatives of Monaco abroad."

" How many servants have I in all, including stable men ? "

" Twenty-five."

" Then you mean to say that there are three hundred and sixty-one persons employed under the crown for a population of thirteen hundred male inhabitants of full age ?"

"Yes, Sir, and M. Blanc employs on his works and at the Casino eight hundred of the remainder."

This was a startling state of things, but I soon found out that, as Colonel Jacquemet had used his men twice over on my arrival, so we used our politicians twice or thrice, politicians being happily scarce with us. Many posts were filled by one man, a plan which has its advantages as well as its drawbacks, the advantages predominating in a country where there are eleven hundred and sixty posts to fill and only thirteen hundred grown male inhabitants.

To give you an idea of the way in which we used our men, Baron Imberty, our Governor-General for instance, was also President of the Council of State, Chancellor of the Order of St. Charles, President of the Maritime Council, President of the Board of Public Works, President of the Bureau de Bienfaisance, etc. etc.

Thanks to M. Blanc and his gambling establishment, and thanks to the large private fortune
of my family, the finances of Monaco were in
a flourishing position. Prince Charles had had
half a million of francs a year of private fortune
and of revenue from the gambling tables. My
cousin Albert had had three hundred thousand
francs a year. I consequently had eight hundred
thousand francs of private fortune, or £32,000
a year, out of which I could easily keep up the
palace, the stables, and, if I chose, a powerful
steam yacht, together with my cousin's house in
Belgium as a summer residence. The cost of
the government for army, church, education, and
justice, was two hundred thousand francs a year.
Public works were dealt with liberally by M.
Blanc as a part of his "concession." The ordinary revenue was derived from four sources, each
contributing about an equal share. These were :—

I. The payment of the Government of France for half the value of the tobacco sold in the principality on behalf of the French *régie*.

II. The payment of France for customs collected by France in my ports.

III. The payment by the "Paris, Lyons, Méditerranée" Railway for right of passage.

IV. Our only local tax, one on all lands and houses changing hands.

The total receipts were two hundred thousand francs, or about the same as the total expense of government.

I dismissed M. de Payan ; and without telling anyone where I was going. I walked up to the Casino by myself.

I was little known by sight at present in the town, as those who had seen me enter it in uniform and on horseback the day before would hardly recognize me in deep mourning and on foot. I passed unnoticed by the guards, and on reaching the Casino, hot and dusty, was stopped by one of the employés of the bank, I said, "Take me to M. Blanc."

Under similar circumstances the Prince of Wales is introduced as "Captain White," but then he is not a *sovereign* prince; and I preferred to give no name at all than to assume an alias.

I found him literally "a counting out his money." That is to say, two clerks were counting rouleaus of gold while he at a small table was quietly playing patience with two packs of cards. At a bureau was a third clerk, an Englishman, translating into French for his benefit one of Mr. Bagehot's leaders in the *Economist*.

He knew me at once, although he had seen me but for a moment and in a wholly different dress. Bowing low, and speaking not to me but to his clerks, he said, "Qu'on nous laisse." The moment they had left the room he bowed to the ground again, and said, "Ah monseigneur, votre seigneurerie me fait trop d'honneur! J'allais écrire à monsieur le chambellan pour lui demander de vouloir bien solliciter une audience en mon nom, afin de déposer mes respectueux hommages aux pieds de votre Altesse. Elle me comble en venant chez moi incognito."

M. Blanc, whose appearance I described before, is well known to gambling Europe as a distinguished political economist, the keeper of the greatest "hell" on earth, and the loving father of a pair of pretty and accomplished daughters, living upon roulette, but himself innocent now-a-days of all games but the mildest patience— of which he knows sixty kinds. At Monaco he is more than a public character: he is a benefactor and a prince. Attacks may be made upon

gambling establishments even conducted as his
is, but I am disposed to agree with the Jesuit
fathers of the Visitation that the Monaco roulette
—forbidden to the inhabitants of Monaco and of
the neighbouring parts of France—does not do
much harm to anyone, although I could hardly
go with Père Pellico so far as to prohibit the
building of a Protestant church while he tolerates
a " hell," and even permits his students to visit
the musical portion of its rooms. I had no wish
in my proposed reforms to reform out of existence my roulette revenue. I wished indeed to
make good use of it ; better use than my pre-
decessors had done. I wanted to make of Monaco
a Munich and a Dresden all in one. I would
have a gallery of the greatest modern pictures
—great ancient ones are not now to be obtained
—a magnificent orchestra, a theatre of the first
rank ; art, in short, of all kind of the highest

class by which to raise the culture of my people, who, excluded from the gambling side of the Casino by a wise ordinance of my predecessor, would reap the benefit without drinking the poison of the roulette.

I found M. Blanc's mind running upon the question of whether English families would be most attracted to Monaco by pigeon-shooting or by an English church. The church he fancied most, but owing to the opposition of Père Pellico it would have to be built upon the hill a mile off from the Casino, in the territory of France.

"I will authorise you to disregard Père Pellico's bigotry, and to build it where you please," I cried.

M. Blanc smiled, and said, "If your Serene Highness will excuse me, I had sooner not go against the Jesuits."

I wasn't king in my own country, as it

appeared. Expel the Jesuits, the tempter within
me suggested; but then I wasn't Bismarck, and
I hadn't a "national liberal" party at my back.

I rapidly exposed my views to M. Blanc. I
was much struck by the fact that his practical
mind insisted on viewing my reforms as ques-
tions not of principles but of men.

"You have no men to back you," he kept
saying; "and if you turn out your present set
and get some clever Germans you will be deposed." He had dropped the excessive formality
of speech with which he had begun. Several
times he used the phrase, "Dr. Coulon is the
only man you have." Then, after thinking for
a time, "What do you propose to gain by your
reforms? You are rich. Your people are con-
tented. Why trouble yourself? As for works of
art, as for theatre, as for orchestra, these things
are matters of money, and I will do my best to

help. I am not sure that as a mere investment they will not pay, and at all events I will do my best to make them do so; but as for your reforms of army, church, and education that you talk about, I beg your Highness to leave it all alone. The shares in the bank will fall ten per cent. when it is known. My shares here are like the funds at Paris, they hate liberty. The less liberty, the higher they stand. It is just the same at Paris. Suppress a journal, and the *rente* rise a franc. Suppress all the journals, and they would rise five francs! Suppress the Assembly, and they would rise ten! Does your Serene Highness take part in pigeon-shooting?"

Making nothing of M. Blanc, except as to art matters, I returned slowly to the Castle, where I found the Council of State assembled to take the oaths.

I chatted with the members of the Council,

but arranged to develope my plans in the first place to a few carefully-selected individuals. I fixed hours at which I would receive M. de Payan; Dr. Coulon; the curé of the cathedral; l'Abbé Ramin; Père Pellico; and Colonel Jacquemet; after seeing the Governor General, Baron Imberty, and talking matters over with him. Baron Imberty I only saw because not to see him would be to pass a slight upon him; but I had no hope of help from him, and none from Colonel Jacquemet. From Père Pellico I knew that I should meet with opposition, and I received him only to see how strong and of what nature the opposition would be. I built my hopes upon M. de Payan, Dr. Coulon, and l'Abbé Ramin.

To Baron Imberty I said only that I contemplated a reform in the army, a gradual liberation of the church from state control, and the re-organization of the schools. He answered that my wish was law, but that the church was very well as she stood.

To Colonel Jacquemet I explained in detail my military re-organization scheme, which was the best of my reforms. I pointed out to him that his force of forty men, now reduced to thirty-eight by the unfortunate wart and cold, was only preserved from becoming the laughing-stock of Europe by its exceptional discipline and courage. It was absolutely necessary for me to say this or he would have had a fit upon the spot. I directed that a list should be prepared of all the male inhabitants aged from sixteen to thirty, and numbering, as I calculated, about eight hundred. That of them those physically fit—some six hundred, as I should suppose—were to receive drill, and ultimately uniforms. The gallant forty men were to become sergeants, corporals, and inferior officers of the new national regiment. Captain Ruggeri and Lieutenant Gasignol were named its majors, and Lieutenants Plati and De la Rosière the senior captains. Four other captains were to be selected from among the privates and non-commissioned officers of the guard. The new levy was to be unpaid, and the only increased expense would be the uniforms and rifles, and at first the additional pay of the ten new officers. As vacancies occurred in company officers they were to be filled up by election by the company, but the majors were to be appointed by the colonel. The cost of the uniforms and arms I proposed to meet by selling for old iron our twenty magnificent, but useless pieces of old artillery. Modern artillery for the fortress I proposed to provide out of my private income, and as defence of the town was our only possible service, of field artillery I decided to have none. The night sentry duty at the palace was to be performed by the paid sergeants only, and the regiment was to parade but once a week. I could see that Colonel Jacquemet did not like it, but he bowed and left the room.

My next interview was with M. de Payan. He heartily concurred in my army reform, and said that no measure could be better for the country, educationally, than my plan of universal service of this limited character. When I came to talk of church reforms, however, M. de Payan was very cold and hard to fire. He advised me to talk the matter over with the curé, l'Abbé Ramin, a most moderate man, and to beware of Father Pellico. From this negative position I could not move him.

The curé was my next visitor. He also agreed heartily in the wisdom of my army reform. He listened without dissent to my proposal for the gradual cessation of the small grant to the priests, including that to himself. On the other hand, when I spoke about the necessity of procuring lay teachers for the schools, he began to weep. I changed the subject, and when I allowed him to leave the room he said, with a singularly sweet smile, that he would go with my reforms as far ¨as he could, that so just a man as my Highness would not harm his country, that God would watch over his church. - I was touched by Abbé Ramin.

Dr. Coulon was then shown in. A man of intellect, as I could see at the first glance. I set before him my army reform, and he was delighted with it. I touched upon the separation of church and state, and he said that it was not hard to be done at Monaco—in name, that is, but difficult indeed to be done in fact. Still he supposed the name of separation was what I wanted, and the gradual cessation of the stipends, which would put Monaco in accord with the modern movement. I then referred to education.

He shook his head, and answered, "I should be your Highness's sole supporter, and I am a materialist, and only tolerated here on account of my medical skill, and placed on the Council of Education because, as I am not in the habit of running my head against stone walls, I always side with the Jesuits."

I insisted on the vast improvement in the standard of secular education to be expected from the introduction of highly trained lay teachers, and said that the priests should be absolutely free to teach the children out of school hours.

His reply was a singular one, and shook me.

"Your Highness is a democrat," he said. "How then can your Highness impose your will in this matter upon a people who are unanimous? If your Highness wishes to escape individual responsibility for the existence of the present state of things, your Highness can dissolve the council of state and institute an elective parliament. That parliament would consist, let us say, of twelve members. If so, eleven would be priests or Jesuits, and the twelfth M. Blanc of the Casino —a body which would resemble in complexion some of the school boards in your Highness's favourite England. Your Highness has a heavy task, and if that task be persevered in, I fear that the state of your Highness's nerves will be such as to require my prescriptions."

He was very free in his conversation, the old doctor, but it was a pleasing change after Baron

Imberty and M. de Payan ; not but what Abbé
Ramin had much attracted me.

I did my best to charm Père Pellico. I
courted him as my other subjects courted me.
He was expansive in manner ; but I am not a
fool, and though only twenty-four, I knew enough
of human nature to see that there was another
Père Pellico underneath the smiling case-work
which talked to me. To my military reform he
had no objection, provided I exempted Jesuit
students from service. I answered that I would
exempt all those at present in Monaco, to
which he replied that he feared then that
I should never have the pleasure of seeing
any others. I thought to myself "here is"
— but Père Pellico smiled and slowly spoke
again.

"Your Highness was thinking, I venture to
imagine, that that would be an additional reason

for hurrying your military reform. But I must crave the pardon of your Highness for speaking except in reply to your Highness. I have not the habit of courts."

I spoke then of the Church ; he was indifferent—the salaries of his four professors could easily be got from Italy. I then touched upon education.

Père Pellico, to my astonishment, exclaimed, " But on the contrary ; my opinions are *not* different from those of your Highness. They are the same. But as a democrat I do not venture, although I may be wrong, to force them upon the people."

Here was a change of base.

" If I were your Highness," he continued, " I would dismiss the Council of State and call an elected parliament to frame a constitution. That would be a more regular method of proceeding than limiting your own prerogative by the exercise of that very prerogative itself."

" Father," I replied, " is not the country somewhat small for the complicated machinery of parliament ? "

" Why then not try a Plebiscite, ' yes ' or ' no,' upon certain written propositions, as in Zurich ? "

" How liberal a politician can afford to be when he has the people with him," I thought to myself as I bowed out Father Pellico.

For the next three weeks, until the end of February, things went smoothly with me. My great aunt bothered me so to marry a " nice steady young lady who would maintain the dignity of the Court, check the extravagance of the steward, and count the linen," that I got Dr. Coulon to tell her that she would die unless she removed to Nice. She preferred a short remove to a long one, and took herself off to my great relief. She was a very fussy, but a clever and a really good old lady. My army reform went well enough, and the church edict was fulminated without meeting with opposition. I bought, through Mr. Gambart, who often came to Nice, a charming Leighton and a glorious Watts, and a fine Verboeckhoven from M. Blanc, as a beginning of the public collection. I moved the councils to the palace, and fitted up the public offices thus rendered vacant as my museum. I got M. Lucas at the Casino to improve his already admirable orchestra, to start a free school for instrumental music, and to play once a week in the town of Monaco instead of at Monte Carlo. I wrote to M. Gounod, whom I had the honour to count among my friends, to offer him the Louis Quinze rooms beyond the Chambre d'York, at the north-west corner of the Castle, with the most lovely view in both directions,

and the prettiest decorations to my mind in all
the palace, if he would come and stay with me
as a permanent visitor, and countenance our
musical efforts. I founded a school for model-
ling in clay, a class in decorative art which I
taught myself, and I made the arrangements for
the reception of a troop of actors in the winter,
and for the production of Gounod's " Jeanne
d'Arc "—a piece which was suggested by Père
Pellico. In the palace itself I made many im-
provements. Of the Chambre d'York I left
nothing but the pretty mosaic floor, but the
room itself, which had been gilt from top to
bottom, bed and all, by my great-grandfather to
take out the taste of the Great French Revolution,
during which the palace had been a poor-house,
I turned into a meeting room for the Council
of State. My steam yacht had come with a
temporary crew of English tars, and my two

great 15-inch 60-ton Krupp guns—one for the terrace, seawards, and one for the garden, landwards—were ordered. The "reports" had been abolished; the nagging surveillance of the police had been abolished; the Church establishment had been abolished; and I then had nothing left to abolish but myself, the abolition of myself being a measure from which I shrank although, like King Leopold, I was ready to go if my subjects wished it.

The only one of my reforms which was really popular was the national army, which afforded all the young married men in the principality a weekly holiday away from their wives. But Major Gasignol, who had a "soul above buttons," used on parade when he was acting as adjutant to take an opportunity of reminding me of the days of glory when one of my ancestors, Grimaldi II., about the time of the Norman conquest of England, had delivered at Rome the Pope from the forces of no less a personage than the Emperor.

All this time, however, my education scheme and my substitution of an elective for a nominated council were in abeyance, the first on account of Père Pellico's opposition, the second I might almost say on account of his support.

Dr. Coulon, consulted by me, often used to say, "Why does not your Highness throw the responsibility upon a parliament of leaving matters where they are?"

"But I wish to change them," I as often replied.

"I can understand that your Highness should wish to be thought to wish to change them, but further than that point I can not follow your Highness."

I seriously thought of clapping Dr. Coulon

into prison for his impertinence, but then he was the only liberal in Monaco, and I was a liberal prince. How I wished, though, that my uncle had not been such a fool as to invite the Jesuits, harassed in Italy in 1862, to take refuge in his dominions.

I was no further advanced than my grandfather, Florestan I., who when overtaken by the events of 1848, which lost him Mentone and Roquebrune, contemplated a parliament, which however he never formed. It was a funny constitution was that one which he posted on the walls, and over which I had often mused. It had not gone further than being posted on the walls, I should add, because my grandfather found that it would not bring back Mentone, and as he was strong enough to keep Monaco with or without it he had, very sensibly, put it in the fire. The 11th article of it was the oddest :—" La presse sera libre, mais sujette à des lois répressivés." But the *first* article gave the tone to the whole :—" The sole religion of the State is the Catholic, Apostolic, Roman."

I strolled up the terraces of Monte Carlo, which always reminded me of John Martin's idea of heaven, and consulted M. Blanc. He was in especially good humour that day, because " Madame Brisebanque" and " the Maltese" had both been losing money. Still, when I talked of my parliament and my education reform, he talked of " Jacob's ladder" and of other infallible systems of ruining him which never had any result except that of beggaring their authors. He told me a long-winded story of how at Homburg a company called " La Contrebanque" had won twenty-four days in succession, and how on the twenty-fifth they had sent for a watchman and an iron chest to guard their winnings, how that afternoon their secretary had lost the whole capital in eighteen *coups*, and how the innocent watchman had marched up and down all night religiously guarding an empty chest. I tried to hark back to my subject, when off he went again at a tangent, and told me how the day before on opening the " bienfaisance " collection-box in the hall of the hotel they had found no money, but all the letters of an American gentleman who had posted them there the year before. Another of his anecdotes was of a lady who, having lost, had eaten a thousand-franc note on a slice of bread and butter to improve her luck. M. Blanc left the Casino in his carriage just after I had ridden off, and without seeming to look I saw well enough out of the corner of my eyes after he had passed me on the road, that the people uncovered to him more universally and for a longer time than to myself. There was, how-

ever, one difference between us—I returned the
bows and he did not.

I gave up M. Blanc and pursued my reforming course, abandoning, however, the idea of a
parliament and fearing to touch education. My
government, now in working order, resembled in
no way that which you English think the best
of all possible polities—" constitutional monarchy "
—which with you appears to me to mean a
democratic republic tempered by snobbism and
corruption. Mine was a socialistic autocracy,
which, in spite of my failure, I maintain to be
the best of governments, provided only that you
can secure the best of autocrats.

I had no one to back me in what I did.
Major Gasignol and some of the other officers
were strongly favourable to the army reform,
which gave them service and promotion. Dr.
Coulon was half favourable to my views, and a

quarter favourable to my ways of working them
out in action. L'Abbé Ramin was conciliatory
and kind. M. de Payan was grimly neutral.
Every other functionary was an active, though
veiled, enemy to nine-tenths of my proposals.
The people were abjectly passive, and I almost
wished that the auberge of the " *Crapaud
Volant* " of *Rabagas* had had a real existence.
At last, however, I conjured up the spirit to
found a school with lay teachers, arranging to
pay its cost over and above the expected fees
out of my own purse. No one came to it, and
the Jesuit schools and the schools of the *frères
de la doctrine* continued to be thronged. The
Catholic schools were supported by the state.
Mine were supported by myself. I went a step
further, and I offered Father Pellico the alterna-
tives of stopping the state contributions to all
schools, or of continuing them, provided that lay

teachers only were employed during the principal hours of the day. He coldly said that an agreement of the nature proposed by me would be contrary to his duty, and that if I chose to stop the state contributions to his schools the effect of my action would be to shake my throne without harming them. He added that if he was to go to prison he was at the service of my officer of the guard. I replied that he was welcome to his opinion.

The next day the edict appeared. It was countersigned by Baron Imberty, who disapproved of it, but not by M. de Payan, who had resigned and left for Nice to consult the Bishop. As I drove through the town in the afternoon, I was coldly received by the people, and the proclamation was torn down on the following night. The weekly parade of the militia was put off for fear of a hostile demonstration; and on the day on which it would have taken place I received, instead of the muster-roll of the national regiment, a vote of thanks from the Executive Committee of the English National Education League, and notice of my unanimous election to membership of the Council of that body.

A strange event occurred in the afternoon, (it was the 11th of March), to distract my thoughts. General Garibaldi, who had been travelling *incognito*, and with the permission of the French Government, given conditionally on the *incognito* being strictly preserved, to visit his birthplace—Nice, applied to me to know whether I would receive him if he stopped at Monaco for a day on his return. I replied that I should be glad to see him, the more so as I had met his son Ricciotti at Greenwich in June 1870, at the dinner of the Cobden Club, to which orgie he and I had both been lured

by the solicitations of the arch-gastronomist, the
jovial Mr. T. B. Potter. I did not add that
our acquaintance had been interrupted by the
war in which the same clever and conceited
officer had cut up my cousin's (the King of
Wurtemberg) troops at Châtillon-sur-Seine.

On the 12th the old General came, and I
met him at the station and drove him to the
palace. The news that he was with me soon
spread through the town, and a mob collected
at the palace gates. The General, to whom I
had given the "bishop's rooms," which had once
been occupied by Monseigneur Dupanloup, his
arch enemy, imagined that the crowd was com-
posed of his admirers, and, leaning upon his
stick, he proceeded to harangue them from the
window of the private apartments. Some hun-
dreds of my subjects, I was afterwards informed,
had listened to him languidly enough until he

r

began to attack the Jesuits, when arose the
uproar which brought me to his room, and all
my household into the courtyard. I begged him
to remember where he was, but the howling of
the mob had excited the old lion, and the more
they threatened the more violently he declaimed.
When he was pulled into a chair by Major
Gasignol the mischief was done, and a maddened
crowd was raging on the *place* crying "à bas
Garibaldi," "à bas les Communistes," "à bas le
Prince."

Colonel Jacquemet made his way to me and
said, "Sir, I can count on twenty of the sergeants and corporals who are in the courtyard,
ex-soldiers of your Highness's ex-garde. They
are grand old soldiers, and with the strong
walls to help them will hold, this *canaille* in
check."

He might have said, "Sir, I don't like your

ways, and have disapproved of everything that
you have done, but after all you are the right-
ful Prince of Monaco, as well as a good fellow,
saving your Highness's presence, and I am ready
to die for you." He didn't. He only spoke
the words that I have set down.

My answer was an unhesitating one.

" I, Prince Florestan the Reformer, am not
going to hold my throne by force if I can't hold
it by love ; and, moreover, if I wished to do so
it is doubtful whether I could succeed."

As I spoke the crowd parted asunder, and
I saw advancing through it in a wedge the
English blue-jackets from my yacht, armed with
cutlasses. A few stones were thrown at them,
but of these they took not the smallest notice.
At their head was the captain of the port, a
native Monégascan, the very man who years
before had saved my sailor cousin from the

waves. They entered the courtyard, and I at once asked them to make their way, with General Garibaldi in the midst, back to the yacht, and steam with him to Mentone, land him, and return. At the same time I sent for Father Pellico. It was lucky the sailors had come, for I soon discovered that the carbineers had made common cause with the mob, and that the sergeants who were ready to die for me would not have escorted Garibaldi.

The mob howled dismally as he left, but he was embarked safely just before Father Pellico reached the palace gate. I told him that the General had left, and asked him whether this concession would satisfy the crowd. He asked whether I was prepared at the same time to give way about the schools. I told him that if I thought that after doing so I could continue to reign with advantage to the country and credit

to myself I would willingly give way, but that
if he thought that in the event of my abdi-
cation the public peace could be maintained
until a vote was taken to decide the future
of the country, I should prefer to return to
my books and to my boat. He said that he
hoped that I should stop, but that if, on the
other hand, I went he thought that order would
be maintained.

I bowed to him and said, "Père Pellico, you
may if you please occupy the throne of the
Grimaldis. I shall leave in an hour when the
yacht returns."

I went on to the balcony and attempted to
address the crowd. If they would have listened
to a word I said I might have turned them, but
not a syllable could be heard. I could not
" address my remarks to the reporters," because
owing to the wise precautions of my predecessor

with regard to the press there were none. I
retired amid a shower of small stones.

Colonel Jacquemet's language was fearful to
listen to. The air was thick with his curses.
I was reminded of the question of a little girl
friend of mine, who having been taken out one
day to an inspection by the Commander-in-
Chief of the garrison of Portsmouth upon South-
sea common, asked on her return home if "the
Duke of Cambridge wasn't a very pious man,"
explaining that she had heard him "say his
prayers"—alluding doubtless to His Royal Highness's favourite expression of "God bless my
body and soul!" If he had ever read history
the colonel would have known that the fire-
eating d'Artagnan of "Three Musketeers" re-
nown once commanded the fortress of Monaco
for Louis the Fourteenth, under my ancestor the
Marshal, and he might have been inspired by

a desire to emulate his fame, but, as it was, he
seemed chiefly moved by a loathing for his
tattered fellow-subjects. He wanted to mow
them with grape—of which we had none ; he
wanted to blow them into the air—but to
reason with him was useless, and I was unable
even to fix his attention enough to bid him
farewell.

As I left the palace, surrounded by the tars
and preceded and followed by the sergeants of
the ex-garde, Abbé Ramin came running up and
seized me by the hand.

"Your Serene Highness must not leave us,"
he cried ; "the people are' irritated for a moment
against their prince, but happier days will
come."

"I can stop if I please, Abbé Ramin," I
replied, "but only either by firing upon the
people, or by blockading them and depriving

the women and children of the upper town of
their daily bread. I will do neither."

"History will speak of your Highness as
your Highness deserves!"

"My dear friend—for I believe you are my
only friend in Monaco—I thank you for coming
to bid me farewell, but don't talk of history,
for history will only declare me to have been
an obstinate young fool."

We moved off slowly down the hill amid
the hisses of the crowd. The sergeants formed
square upon the quay, I embraced Colonel
Jacquemet and the Abbé, stepped into the gig,
and in a minute was on board. Steam was up,
and the next evening I landed at Marseilles.

By a telegram from the Abbé I learnt that
an informal vote of the adult male inhabitants
of the principality had been taken that day,
and that the result was this :—

For Annexation to France $\begin{cases} 1131 - Oui. \\ 1 - Non. \end{cases}$

The *Non* was M. Blanc, who, being a Frenchman, ought not to have been allowed to vote at all. I heard afterwards that on learning my departure he had pronounced the following epitaph upon me :—

"Ah le jeune homme est parti. Je m' y attendais. Il aimait la liberté celui là."

The Casino is removed to Cairo, and M. Blanc's eldest daughter is to marry the Viceroy's youngest son.

My tutor at Cambridge received me with a solemn face ; but I laughingly exclaimed, "You see, Sir, after all I did want an *exeat*, even if an *absit* would not have done."

The only later news that I have to record is a letter from my friend Gambetta, promising that when he becomes President of France I

shall be préfêt of the Department of the Alpes
Maritimes, which includes my ex-dominions, on
condition that I am very moderate.

END.

There is no moral that can be drawn from
my fall applicable to the present state of English
politics. This may be seen indeed from the
comments of the only three English papers of
last Friday and Saturday that noticed it. The
Morning Advertiser, which, Tory as it is, prefers
Radical-Orangeism to Tory-Popery (and beer to
both), classed me along with the Tichborne
claimant as a victim to the Jesuits, whereas I
wasn't a victim at all; and if I had been,
should have been a victim to my own obstinacy,
as I certainly could have stopped at Monaco if
I had pleased to do so—either by raising a
popular clamour against the priests, which would

have been immoral, or by accepting Père Pellico's
conditions, which would have been humiliating.
The *National Reformer*, the organ of Mr. Bradlaugh, patted me on the back as an ill-used
republican ; and the *Standard* said that my fall
showed the absolute necessity of maintaining the
25th clause of the Education Act intact, which
is what I could not for the life of me see. On
the contrary, so opposite are the conditions of
England and of Monaco, that what would have
succeeded in one would have failed in the other
as a matter of course. In England you have a
divided church ; an increasing and active though
still little numerous Catholic body ; a materialistic
world of fashion which goes alternately to Mr.
Wilkinson and Canon Liddon, Mr. Haweis and
Mr. Stopford Brooke, and does not believe a word
that any of them says—unless it is Mr. Haweis,
but then, doctrinally speaking, he says nothing.

You have the old nonconformist bodies, able and powerful still, though less powerful than before 1868; and you have the Wesleyans, pulpy but rich. Outside of them all you have people who believe two-thirds of them in the Bible pure and simple, but with prominence given in their minds to the communistic side of the New Testament, and one-third in nothing unless it is Mr. Charles Watts, Mr. Austin Holyoake, and Mr. Bradlaugh. The most flourishing publications in your country are *Zadkiel's Almanac* and *Reynolds' Newspaper*, belonging to the opposite poles, but equally at war with all that is most powerful and rich and respectable in your society. What resemblance is there in this state of things, full of life but wholly wanting in unity, to that at Monaco, dead, but single in faith? At Monaco all that believed—and most believed—were earnest Catholics, wielded for political purposes by one man. Had my parliamentary scheme been carried out the cumulative vote would have been inoperative, and Mr. Hare had he been there would have hanged himself from the castle flag-staff, for there was no minority. As in East Prussia the peasants, suddenly presented with universal suffrage by Von Bismarck and asked for whom they would vote, said with one accord, "For the King."— "You can't "—"Then for the Crown Prince "— so at Monaco the population would have replied "for Père Pellico."

All the same there is a moral to be drawn from my fall, and it applies to the French Republic. I conjure my friends of the French radical party not to let radicalism in France be bound up with indecent speeches made over the graves at "civil funerals," or with the denial of the Immortality of the Soul. In England, in spite of occasional attempts of the *Standard* to couple "atheists" and "republicans," no such warning is needed; but in France it comes almost too late. No system of government can be permanent which has for its opponents all the women in the country, and for supporters only half the men; and any party will have for opponents all the women which couples the religious question with the political and the social, and raises the flag of materialism. Women are not likely to abandon the idea of a compensation in the next world for the usage which too many of them meet with in this.

As for my failure at Monaco, I went too fast. I agree with Mr. Freeman, your English historian, that a sudden breach in the continuity of national institutions is an evil, and that "the witness of history teaches us that, in changing a long established form of executive government, the more gently and warily the work is done the more likely it is to be lasting." I could have stopped at Monaco by humbling myself, but at all events I went too fast. If they take me back, which I really think for their own sakes they had better do, I will go much slower. But I have no time to write any more, for I have been put without training into the first boat, and we are to stop up during the greater portion of the Easter "vac.," as we have a capital chance of "keeping head."

LONDON: R. CLAY, SONS, AND TAYLOR, PRINTERS.